CALIFORNIA
NATIVE AMERICAN TRIBES

OHLONE TRIBE

by
Mary Null Boulé

Illustrated by
Daniel Liddell

Merryant Publishers, Inc.
Vashon, WA 98070

This series is dedicated to Virginia Harding, whose editing
expertise and friendship brought this project to fruition.

Library of Congress Catalog Card Number: 92-61897

ISBN: 1-877599-38-7

Copyright © 1992, Merryant Publishing

7615 S.W. 257th St., Vashon, WA 98070.

FOREWORD

Native American people of the United States are often living their lives away from major cities and away from what we call the mainstream of life. It is, then, interesting to learn of the important part these remote tribal members play in our everyday lives.

More than 60% of our foods come from the ancient Native American's diet. Farming methods of today also can be traced back to how tribal women grew crops of corn and grain. Many of our present day ideas of democracy have been taken from tribal governments. Even some 1,500 Native American words are found in our English language today.

Fur traders bought furs from tribal hunters for small amounts of money, sold them to Europeans and Asians for a great deal of money, and became rich. Using their money to buy land and to build office buildings, some traders started business corporations which are now the base of our country's economy.

There has never been enough credit given to these early Americans who took such good care of our country when it was still in their care. The time has come to realize tribal contributions to our society today and to give Native Americans not only the credit, but the respect due them.

Mary Boulé

A-frame cradle for girls; tule matting. Tubatulabal tribe.

GENERAL INFORMATION

Creation legends told by today's tribal people speak of how, very long ago, their creator placed them in a territory, where they became caretakers of that land and its animals. None of their ancient legends tells about the first Native Americans coming from another continent.

It is important to respect the different beliefs and theories, to learn from and seek the truth in all of them.

Villagers' tribal history lessons do not agree with the beliefs of anthropologists (scientific historians who study the habits and customs of humans).

Clues found by these scientists lead them to believe that ancient tribespeople came to North America from Asia during the Ice Age period some 20 to 35 thousand years ago. They feel these humans walked over a land strip in the Bering Straits, following animal herds who provided them with food.

Scientists' understanding of ancient people must come from studying clues; for example, tools, utensils, baskets, garbage discoveries, and stories they passed from one generation to the next.

California's Native Americans did not organize into large tribes. Instead they divided into tribelets, sometimes having as many as 250 people. Some tribelets had only one chief for each village.

From 20 to 100 people could be living in one village, which usually had several houses. In most cases, these groups of people were one family and were related to each other. From five to ten people of a family might live in one house. For instance, a mother, a father, two or three children, a grandmother, or aunt or daughter-in-law might live together.

Village members together would own the land important to them for their well-being. Their land might include oak trees with precious acorns, streams and rivers, and plants which were good to eat. Streams and rivers were especially important to a tribe's quality of life. Water drew animals to it; that meant more food for the tribe to eat. Fish were a good source of food, and traveling by boat was often easier than walking long distances. Water was needed in every part of tribal life.

Village and tribelet land was carefully guarded. Each group knew exactly where the boundaries of its land were found. Boundaries were known by landmarks such as mountains or rivers, or they might also be marked by poles planted in the ground. Some boundary lines were marked by rocks, or by objects placed there by tribal members. The size of a territory had to be large enough to supply food to every person living there.

The California tribes spoke many languages. Sometimes villages close together even had a problem understanding one another. This meant that each group had to be sure of the boundaries of other tribes around them when gathering food. It would not be wise to go against the boundaries and the customs of neighbors. The Native Americans found if they respected the boundaries of their neighbors, not so many wars had to be fought. California tribes, in spite of all their differences, were not as warlike as other tribes in our country.

Not only did the California tribes speak different languages, but their members also differed in size. Some tribes were very tall, almost six feet tall. The shortest people came from the Yuki tribe which had territory in what is now Mendocino County. They measured only about 5'2" tall. All Native Americans, regardless of size, had strong, straight black hair and dark brown eyes.

TRADE

Trading between tribes was an important part of life. Inland tribes had large animal hides that coastal tribes wanted. By trading the hides to coastal groups, inland tribes would receive fish and shells, which they in turn wanted. Coastal tribes also wanted minerals and rocks mined in the mountains by inland tribes. Obsidian rock from the northern mountains was especially wanted for arrowheads. There were, as well, several minerals, mined in the inland mountains, which could be made into the colorful body paints needed for religious ceremonies.

Southern tribes particularly wanted steatite from the Gabrielino tribe. Steatite, or soapstone, was a special metal which allowed heat to spread evenly through it. This made it a good choice to be used for cooking pots and flat frying pans. It could be carved into bowls because of its softness and could be decorated by carving designs into it. Steatite came from Catalina Island in the Coastal Gabrielino territory. Gabrielinos found steatite to be a fine trading item to offer for the acorns, deerskins, or obsidian stone they needed.

When people had no items to trade but needed something, they used small strings of shells for money. The small dentalium shells, which came from the far distant Northwest coast, had great value. Strings of dentalia usually served as money in the Northern California tribes, although some dentalia was used in the Central California tribes.

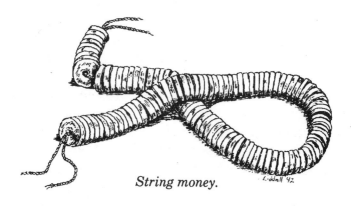

String money.

In southern California clam shells were broken and holes were bored through the center of each piece. Then the pieces were rounded and polished with sandstone and strung into strings for money. These were not thought to be as valuable as dentalia.

Strings of shell money were measured by tattoo marks on the trader's lower arm or hand.

Here is a sample of shell value:

> A house, three strings
> A fishing place, one to three strings
> Land with acorn-bearing oak trees, one to five strings

A great deal of rock and stone was traded among the tribes for making tools. Arrows had to have sharp-edged stone for tips. The best stone for arrow tips was obsidian (volcanic glass) because, when hit properly, it broke off into flakes with very sharp edges. California tribes considered obsidian to be the most valuable rock for trading.

Some tribes had craftsmen who made knives with wooden handles and obsidian blades. Often the handles were decorated with carvings. Such knives were good for trading purposes. Stone mortars and pestles, used by the women for grinding grains into flour, were good trading items.

BASKETS & POTTERY

California tribal women made beautiful baskets. The Pomo and Chumash baskets, what few are left, show us that the women of those tribes might have been some of the finest basketmakers in the world. Baskets were used for gathering and storing food, for carrying babies, and even for hauling water. In emergencies, such as flooding waters, sometimes children, women, and tribal belongings crossed the swollen rivers and streams in huge, woven baskets! Baskets were so tightly woven that not a drop of water could leak from them.

Baskets also made fine cooking pots. Very hot rocks were taken from a fire and tossed around inside baskets with a looped tree branch until food in the basket was cooked.

Most baskets were made to do a certain job, but some baskets were designed for their beauty alone and were excellent for trading. Older women of a tribe would teach young girls how to weave baskets.

Pottery was not used by many California tribes. What little there was seems to have been made by those tribes living near to the Navaho and Mohave tribes of Arizona, and it shows their style. For example, pottery of the California tribes did not have much decoration and was usually a dull red color. Designs were few and always in yellow.

Ohlone hunter wearing deerskin camouflage.

Long thin coils of clay were laid one on top the other. Then the coils were smoothed between a wooden paddle and a small stone to shape the bowl. Pottery from California Native Americans has been described as light weight and brittle (easily broken), probably because of the kind of clay soil found in California.

HUNTING & FISHING

Tribal men spent much of their time making hunting and fishing tools. Bows and arrows were built with great care, to make them shoot as accurately as possible. Carelessly made hunting weapons caused fewer animals to be killed and people then had less food to eat.

Bows made by men of Southern California tribes were made long and narrow. In the northern part of the state bows were a little shorter, thinner, and wider than those of their northern neighbors. Size and thickness of bows depended on the size trees growing in a tribe's territory. The strongest bows were wrapped with sinew, the name given to animal tendons. Sinew is strong and elastic like a rubber band.

Arrows were made in many sizes and shapes, depending on their use. For hunting larger animals, a two-piece arrow was used. The front piece of the arrow shaft was made so that it would remain in the animal, even if the back part was removed or broken off. The arrowhead, or point, was wrapped to the front piece of the shaft. This kind of arrow was also used in wars.

Young boys used a simple wooden arrow with the end sharpened to a point. With this they could hunt small animals like birds and rabbits. The older men of the tribe taught boys how to make their own arrows, how to aim properly, and how to repair broken weapons.

Tribal men spent many hours making and mending fishing nets. The string used in making nets often came from the fibers of plants. These fibers were twisted to make them strong and tough, then knotted into netting. Fences, or weirs, that had one small opening for fish, were built across streams. As the fish swam through the opening they would be caught in netting or harpooned by a waiting fisherman.

Hooks, if used at all, were cut from shells. Mostly hooks could be found when the men fished in large lakes or when catching trout in high mountain areas. Hooks were attached to heavy plant fiber string.

Dip nets, made of netting attached to branches that were bent into a circle, were used to catch fish swimming near shore. Dip nets had long handles so the fishermen could reach deep into the water.

Sometimes a mild poison was placed on the surface of shallow water. This confused the fish and caused them to float to the surface of the water, where they could be scooped up by a waiting fisherman. Not enough poison was used to make humans ill.

Not all fishing was done from the shore. California tribes used two kinds of boats when fishing. Canoes, dug out of one half a log, were useful for river fishing. These were square at each end, round on the bottom, and very heavy. Some of them were well-finished, often even having a carved seat in them.

Today we think of "balsa" as a very lightweight wood, but in

Spanish, the word balsa means "raft". That is why Spanish explorers called the Native American canoes, made from tule reeds, "balsa" boats.

Balsa boats were made of bundled tule reeds and were used throughout most of California. They made into safe, light-weight boats for lake and river use. Usually the balsa canoe had a long, tightly tied bundle of tule for the boat bottom and one bundle for each side of the canoe. The front of the canoe was higher than the back. Balsa boats could be steered with a pole or with a paddle, like a raft.

Men did most of the fishing, women were in charge of gathering grasses, seeds, and acorns for food. After the food was collected, it was either eaten right away or made ready for winter storage.

Except for a few southern groups, California tribes had permanent villages where they lived most of the year. They also had food-gathering places they returned to each year to collect acorns, salt, fish, and other foods not found near their villages.

FOOD

Many different kinds of plant food grew wild in California in the days before white people arrived. Berries and other plant foods grew in the mountains. Forests offered the local tribes everything from pine nuts to animals.

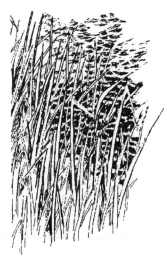

Native Americans found streams full of fish for much of the year. Inland fresh water lakes had large tule reeds growing along their shores. Tule could be eaten as food when plants were young and tender. More important, however, tule was used in making fabric for clothes and for building boats and houses. Tule was probably the most useful plant the California Native Americans found growing wild in their land.

Like all deserts, the one in southern California had little water or fish, but small animals and cactus plants made good food for the local tribes. They moved from place to place harvesting whatever was ripe. Tribal members always knew when and where to find the best food in their territory.

Acorns were the main source of food for all California tribes. Acorn flour was as important to the California Native Americans as wheat is to us today. Five types of California oak trees produced acorns that could be eaten. Those from black oak and tanbark oak seem to have been the favorite kinds.

Since some acorns tasted better than others, the tastiest ones were collected first. If harvest of the favorite acorn was poor some years, then less tasty acorns had to be eaten all winter long.

So important were acorns to California Indians that most tribes built their entire year around them. Acorn harvest marked the beginning of their calendar year. Winter was counted as so many months after acorn harvest, and summer was counted by the number of months before the next acorn harvest.

Acorn harvest ceremonies usually were the biggest events of the year. Most celebrations took place in mid-October and included dancing, feasts, games of chance, and reunions with relatives. Harvest festivals lasted for many days. They were a time of joy for everyone.

The annual acorn gathering lasted two to three weeks. Young boys climbed the oak trees to shake branches; some men used long poles to knock acorns to the ground. Women loaded the nuts into large cone-shaped burden baskets and carried them to a central place where they were put in the sun to dry.

Once the acorns were dried, the women carried them back to the tribe's permanent villages. There they lined special basket-like storage granaries with strong herbs to keep insects away, then stored the acorns inside. Granaries were placed on stilts to keep animals from getting into them and were kept beside tribal houses.

Preparing acorns for each meal was also the women's job. Shells were peeled by hitting the acorns with a stone hammer on an anvil (flat) stone. Meat from the nut was then laid on a stone mortar. A mortar was usually a large stone with a slight dip on its surface. Sometimes the mortar had a bottomless basket, called a hopper, glued to its top. This kept the acorn meat from sliding off the mortar as it was beaten. The meat was then pounded with a long stone pestle. Acorn flour was scraped away from the hopper's sides with a soaproot fiber brush during this process.

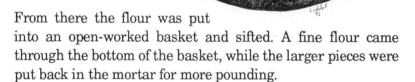

From there the flour was put into an open-worked basket and sifted. A fine flour came through the bottom of the basket, while the larger pieces were put back in the mortar for more pounding.

The most important process came after the acorn flour was sifted. Acorn flour has a very bitter-tasting tannin in it. This bitter taste was removed by a method called leaching. Many tribes leached the flour by first scooping out a hollow in sand near water. The hollow was lined with leaves to keep the flour from washing away. A great deal of hot water was poured through the flour to wash out (leach) the bitterness. Sometimes the flour was put into a basket for the leaching process, instead of using sand and leaves.

Finally the acorn flour was ready to be cooked. To make mush, heated stones were placed in the basket with the flour. A looped tree branch or two long sticks were used to toss the hot rocks around so the basket would not burn. When the mush had boiled, it could be eaten. If the flour and water mixture was baked in an earthen oven, it became a kind of bread. Early explorers wrote that it was very tasty.

Historians have estimated that one family would eat from 1500 to 2000 pounds of acorn flour a year. One reason California native Americans did not have to plant seeds and raise crops was because there were so many acorns for them to harvest each year.

Whether they ate fish or shellfish or plant food or animal meat, nature supplied more than enough food for the Native Americans who lived in California long ago. Many believed their good fortune in having fine weather and plenty to eat came from being good to their gods.

RELIGION

Tribal members had strong beliefs in the power of spirits or gods around them. Each tribe was different, but all felt the importance of never making a spirit angry with them. For that reason a celebration to thank the spirit-gods for treating them well, took place before each food gathering and before each hunting trip, and after each food harvest.

Usually spiritual powers were thought to belong to birds or animals. Most California tribespeople felt bears were very wicked and should not be eaten. But Coyote seems to have been a kind leader who helped them if they were in trouble, even though he seems to have been a bit naughty at times. Eagle was thought to be very powerful and good to native Americans. In some tribes, Eagle was almost as powerful as Sun.

Tribes placed importance on different gods, according to the tribe's needs. Rain gods were the most important spirits to desert tribes. Weather gods, who might bring less rain or warmer temperatures, were important to northern tribes. A great many groups felt there were gods for each of the winds: North, South, East and West. The four directions were usually included in their ceremonial dances and were used as part of the decorations on baskets, pots, and even tools.

Animals were not only worshipped and believed to be spirit-gods, like Deer or Antelope, but tribal members felt there was a personal animal guardian for each one of them. If a tribal member had a deer as guardian, then that person could never kill a deer or eat deer meat.

California Native Americans believed in life after death. This made them very respectful of death and very fearful of angering a dead person. Once someone died, the name of the dead person could never again be said aloud. Since it was easy to accidentally say a name aloud, the name was usually given to a new baby. Then the dead person would not become angry.

Shamans were thought to be the keepers of religious beliefs and to have the ability to talk directly to spirit-gods. It was the job of a village shaman to cure sick people, and to speak to the gods about the needs of the people. Some tribes had several kinds of shamans in one village. One shaman did curing, one scared off evil spirits, while another took care of hunters.

Not all shamans were nice, so people greatly feared their power. However, if shamans had no luck curing sick people or did not bring good luck in hunting, the people could kill them. Most shamans were men, but in a few tribes, women were doctors.

Most California tribal myths have been lost to history because they were spoken and never written down. The legends were told and retold on winter nights around the home fires. Sadly, these were forgotten after the missionaries brought Christianity to California and moved tribal members into the missions.

A few stories still remain, however. It is thought by historians that northwest California tribes were the only ones not to have a myth on how they were created. They did not feel that the world was made and prepared for human beings. Instead, their few remaining stories usually tell of mountain peaks or rivers in their own territory.

The central California tribes had creation stories of a great flood where there was only water on earth. They tell of how man was made from a bit of mud that a turtle brought up from the bottom of the water.

Many southwest tribes believed there was a time of no sky or water. They told of two clouds appearing which finally became Sky and Earth.

Throughout California, however, all tribes had myths that told of Eagle as the leader, Coyote as chief assistant, and of less powerful spirits like Falcon or Hawk.

Costumes for religious ceremonies often imitated these animals they worshipped or feared. Much time was spent in making the dance costumes as beautiful as possible. Red woodpecker feathers were so brilliant a color they were used to decorate religious headdresses, necklaces, or belts. Deerskin clothing was fringed so shell beads could be attached to each thin strip of leather.

Eagle feathers were felt to be the most sacred of religious objects. Sometimes they were made into whole robes.

Religious feather charm.

Usually, though, the feathers were used just for decorations. All these costumes were valuable to the people of each tribe. The village chief was in charge of taking care of the costumes, and there was terrible punishment for stealing them. Clothing worn everyday was not fancy like costuming for rituals.

Willow bark skirt.

CLOTHING

Central and southern California's fine weather made regular clothes not really very important to the Native Americans. The children and men went naked most of the year, but most women wore a short apron-like skirt. These skirts were usually made in two pieces, front and back aprons, with fringes cut into the bottom edges. Often the skirt was made from the inner bark of trees, shredded and gathered on a cord. Sometimes the skirt was made from tule or grass.

In northern California and in rainy or windy weather elsewhere in the state, animal-skin blankets were worn by both men and women. They were used like a cape and wrapped around the body. Sometimes the cape was put over one shoulder and under the other arm, then tied in front. All kinds of skins were used; deer, otter, wildcat, but sea-otter fur was thought to be the best. If the skin was from a small animal, it was cut into strips and woven together into a fabric. At night the cape became a blanket to keep the person warm.

Because of the rainy weather in northern California, the women wore basket caps all the time. Women of the central and south tribes wore caps only when carrying heavy loads, where the forehead had to be used as support. Then a cap helped keep too much weight from being placed on the forehead.

Most California people went barefoot in their villages. For journeys into rough land, going to war, wood gathering, or in colder weather, the tribesmen in central and northwest California wore a one-piece soft shoe with no extra sole, which went high up on the leg.

Southern California tribespeople, however, wore sandals most of the time, wearing high, soled moccasins only when they traveled long distances or into the mountains. Leggings of skin were worn in snow, and moccasins were sometimes lined with grass for more comfort and warmth.

VILLAGE LIFE

Houses of the California tribes were made of materials found in their area. Usually they were round with domed roofs. Except for a few tribes, a house floor was dug into the earth a few feet. This was wise, for it made the home warmer in winter and cooler in summer. It also meant that less material was needed to make house walls.

Framework for the walls was made from bendable branches tied to support poles. Some frames of the houses were covered with earth and grass. Others were covered with large slabs of redwood or pine bark. Central California

Split-stick clapper, rhythm instrument. Hupa tribe.

villagers made large woven mats of tule reed to cover the tops and sides of houses. In the warmer southern area, brush and smaller pieces of bark were used for house walls.

Most California Native American villages had a building called a sweathouse, where the men could be found when they were not hunting, fishing or traveling. It was a very important place for the men, who used it rather like a clubhouse. They could sweat and then scrape themselves clean with curved ribs of deer. The sweathouse was smaller than a family house. Normally it had a center pole framework with a firepit on the ground next to the pole. When the fire was lit, some smoke was allowed to escape through a hole at the top of the roof; however, most was trapped inside the building. Smoke and heat were the main reasons for having a sweathouse. Both were believed to be a way to purify tribal members' bodies. Sweathouse walls were mainly hard-packed earth. The heat produced was not a steam heat but came from a wood-fed fire.

In the center of most villages was a large house that often had no walls, just a roof held up with poles. It was here that religious dances and rituals were held, or visitors were entertained.

Dances were enjoyed and were performed with great skill. Music, usually only rhythm instruments, accompanied the dances. For some reason California Native Americans did not use drums to create rhythms for their dances. Three different kinds of rattles were used by California tribes.

One type, split-clap sticks, created rhythm for dancing. These were usually a length of cane (a hollow stick) split in half lengthwise for about two-thirds of its length. The part still uncut was tightly wound with cord so it would not split all the way. The stick was held at the tied end in one hand and hit against the palm of the other hand to make its sound.

19

A pebble-filled moth cocoon made rhythm for shaman duties. These could range from calling on spirits to cure illnesses, to performing dances to bring rain. Probably the best sounds to beat rhythm for songs and dances came from bundles of deer hooves tied together on a stick. These rattles have a hollow, warm sound.

The only really "musical" instrument found in California was a flute made of reed that was played by blowing across the edge of one end. Melodies were not played on any of these instruments. Most North American Indians sang their songs rather than playing melodies on music instruments.

Special songs were sung for each event. There were songs for healing sick people, songs for success in hunting, war, or marriage. Women sang acorn-grinding songs and lullabies. Songs were sung in sorrow for the dead and during story-telling times. Group singing, with a leader, was the favorite kind of singing. Most songs were sung by all tribe members, but religious songs had to be sung by a special group. It was important that sacred songs not be changed through the years. If a mistake was made while singing sacred music, the singer could be punished, so only specially trained singers would sing ritual songs.

All songs were very short, some of them only 20 to 30 seconds long. They were made longer by repeating the melodies over and over, or by connecting several songs together. Songs usually told no story, just repeated words or phrases or syllables in patterns.

Song melodies used only one or two notes and harmony was never added. Perhaps that is why mission Indians, at those missions with musician priests, especially loved to sing harmony in the church choirs.

Songs and dances were good methods of passing rich tribal traditions on to the children. It was important to tribal adults that their children understand and love the tribe's heritage.

Children were truly wanted by parents in most tribes and new parents carefully watched their tiny babies day and night, to be sure they stayed warm and dry. Usually a newborn was strapped into a cradle and tied to the mother's back so she could continue to work, yet be near the baby at all times. In some tribes, older children took care of babies of cradle age during the day to give the mother time to do all her work, while grandmothers were often in charge of caring for toddlers.

Children were taught good behavior, traditions, and tribal rules from babyhood, although some tribes were stricter than others. Most of the time parents made their children obey. Young children could be lightly punished, but in many tribes those over six or seven years old were more severely punished if they did not follow the rules.

Just as children do today, Native American youngsters had childhood traditions they followed. For instance, one tribal tradition said that when a baby tooth came out, a child waited until dusk, faced the setting sun and threw the tooth to the west. There is no mention of a generous tooth fairy, however.

Tribal parents were worried that their offspring might not be strong and brave. Some tribes felt one way to make their children stronger was by forcing them to bathe in ice cold water, even in wintertime. Every once in a while, for example, Modoc children were awakened from sleep and taken to a cold lake or stream for a freezing bath.

But if freezing baths at night were hard on young Native Americans, their days were carefree and happy. Children were allowed to play all day, and some tribes felt children did not even have to come to dinner if they didn't want to. In those tribes, children could come to their houses to eat anytime of the day.

The games boys played are not too different from those played today. Swimming, hide and seek among the tule reeds, a form of tetherball with a mud ball tied to a pole, and willow-javelin throwing kept boys busy throughout the day.

Fathers made their sons small bows and arrows, so boys spent much time trying to improve their hunting skills. They practised shooting at frogs or chipmunks. The first animal any boy killed was not touched or eaten by him. Others would carry the kill home to be cooked and eaten by villagers. This tradition taught boys always to share food.

Another hunting tool for boys was a hollowed-out willow branch. This became like a modern day beanshooter, only the Native American boys shot juniper berries instead of beans. Slingshots made good hunting weapons, as well.

Girls and boys shared many games, but girls playing with each other had contests to see who could make a basket the fastest, or they played with dolls made of tule. Together, young boys and girls played a type of ring-around-the-rosie game, climbed mountains, or built mud houses.

As children grew older, the boys followed their fathers and the girls followed their mothers as the adults did their daily work. Children were not trained in the arts of hunting or basketmaking, however, until they became teenagers.

HISTORY

Spanish missionaries, led by Fray Junipero Serra, arrived in California in 1769 to build missions along the coast of California. By 1823, fifty years later, 21 missions had been founded. Almost all of them were very successful, and the Franciscan monks who ran them were proud of how many Native Americans became Christians.

However, all was not as the monks had planned it would be. Native American people had never been around the diseases European white men brought with them. As a result, they had no immunity to such illnesses as measles, small pox, or flu. Too many mission Indians died from white men's diseases.

Historians figure there were 300,000 Native Americans living in California before the missionaries came. The missions show records of 83,000 mission Indians during mission days. By the time the Mexicans took over the missions from the Spanish in 1834, only 20,000 remained alive.

The great California Gold Rush of 1849 was probably another big reason why many of the Native Americans died during that time. White men, staking their claim to tribal lands with gold upon it, thought nothing of killing any California tribesman who tried to keep and protect his territory. Fifty-thousand tribal members died from diseases, bullets, or starvation between the gold Rush Days and 1870. By 1910, only 17,000 California Indians remained.

Although the American government tried to set aside reservations (areas reserved for Native Americans), the land given to the Indians often was not good land. Worse yet, some of the land sacred to tribes, such as burial grounds, was taken over by white people and never given back.

Sadly, mission Indians, when they became Christians, forgot the proud heritage and beliefs they had followed for thousands of years. Many wonderful myths and songs they had passed from one generation to the next, on winter nights so long ago, have been lost forever.

Today some 100,000 people can claim California Native American ancestors, but few pure-blooded tribespeople remain. Our link with the Wanderers, who came from Asia so long ago, has been forever broken.

The bullroarer made a deep, loud sound when whirled above the player's head. Tipai tribe.

Villages were usually built beside a lake, stream, or river. Balsa canoes are on the shore. Tule reeds grow along the edge of the water and are drying on poles on the right side of the picture.

Women preparing food in baskets, sit on tule mats. Tule mats are being tied to the willow pole framework of a house being built by one of the men.

OHLONE TRIBE
(Costanoan)

Nearly 10,000 Native Americans lived around San Francisco Bay when Spanish missionaries built missions there in the late 1700s. Before mission times, fifty separate tribelets lived in permanent villages in this small area. A tribelet was made up of one or more villages, as well as many campsites that were used for food gathering. From eight to twelve different languages were spoken by these groups. Sometimes villages just a few miles apart could not understand each other.

During mission times, the word Costanoan was used as a name for the large group of people who lived there. It was not a name the Indians called themselves. Costanoan came from the Spanish word Costeños, meaning "people of the coast", but Costanoan relatives of today do not like this name.

In 1971 all remaining members of Costanoan tribelets united and took the name of Ohlone(Oh lone' ee) Indian Tribe. This group received ownership of the Ohlone Indian cemetery at Mission San Jose. Ohlone ancestors (long-ago relatives) who died at Mission San Jose are buried there, and it is important to them to own this sacred land.

The name Ohlone has been used in the title of this book because it is the word chosen by these Native Americans to identify their tribes and heritage. When you see the name Costanoan, however, you must remember that Ohlone and Costanoan people are one and the same.

Those who study ancient peoples seem to think the Ohlones moved into the area around San Francisco Bay about 1500 years ago from land near what is now Sacramento. Explorers wrote about the everyday lives of this tribe, which helps us to know some facts about Ohlone heritage.

Ohlone territory went from the northern tip of San Francisco Bay to south of Monterey Bay and went east to the mountains. Each boundary was marked by something like a mountain or a river or a large rock. These people did not ever go onto neighboring tribes' lands. They were not looking for trouble but were mostly peaceful in nature.

THE VILLAGE

Each tribelet had one or more permanent village sites. Ohlones left their villages only at certain times of the year to fish, hunt or to gather plant food. The number of people in a village averaged about 200 but could range from 50 to 500 people.

Village houses were usually domed, or rounded at the top. They were made of woven tule, grass, wild alfalfa, or fern mats. The mats were tied onto a framework of poles which were tied at the top. A few tribelets built cone-shaped houses of redwood bark or split planks.

Houses ranged in size from six feet to twenty feet across at ground level. If more than one family lived together, the house had to be larger. The largest house in a village belonged to the chief. When a house became full of fleas it was burned.

Each village had a small sweathouse for the men and women. Children were not allowed in a sweathouse. Usually the sweathouse was built by digging a pit into the dirt bank of a stream. It was a very small building that could hold only six to eight people. One had to crouch down inside the sweathouse. It was not tall enough for adults to stand up. Even to go in, they had to crouch down on all fours and crawl through a tiny door.

Tribal men kept their hunting and fishing tools in the sweathouse. Flutes and split-stick rhythm clappers were tucked into the rafters. Things like arrow quivers hung on the back wall, and a few steatite stones for making arrows straight could be found on the sweathouse floor. Much work was done here; it was not used just for cleaning the body by sweating.

There was a dance area in the village which was nothing more than a round or oval-shaped piece of ground with a four-foot-high fence of brush all around it. There were two doors into the enclosure, but it had no roof.

A large domed building, usually with walls of thatch (grass mats), was known as the assembly house. This was built big enough for all the villagers to fit inside. It was usually in the center of a village, near the dance enclosure. Family houses were built around the assembly house and dance enclosure.

Scattered about the village were huge baskets on stick legs. These were granaries which stored acorns, the most important food of the Ohlone tribe. At the edge of the village, on a flat piece of ground, was a play field where games were played during free time.

VILLAGE LIFE

While men repaired fish nets and made arrows, the women prepared food for meals or for storage for the coming winter. When the weather was sunny and warm, all women worked together outside the houses. Houses were crowded with belongings and did not give the women much room to work.

Chiefs had to have the largest houses, not only because they were important, but because a chief had to make room for many storage baskets full of food. It was the duty of a chief to meet all strangers and visitors with presents and a feast. Entertaining guests with plenty of good food was an important job of a chief.

In the Ohlone tribelets, a chief could be either a man or a woman. Usually the job went from father to son, but if a chief had no son, a chief's sister or daughter might hold this honor. All the villagers had to approve of a chief before he or she could take office.

Chiefs were wealthy, but they were watched by all the village so that their wealth was used for others, not kept for personal use. The chief's wealth was a public trust to be held for the needs of old people, widows, orphans, and the handicapped. There had to be enough stored food for all the people in the village who could not gather their own food.

A chief was also in charge of setting dates for festivals, dances, religious ceremonies, and such. If a tribe ran low on food, trading beads, or anything else, the chief was blamed by tribal members.

Other jobs of a chief were leading hunts and gatherings for food, and leading war expeditions. A war chief was on the village chief's council. He had power only to determine war methods.

Most wars had to do with two tribes not agreeing on territory boundaries. Warfare was done two ways. Either a surprise attack was used, or a fight could be pre-arranged. Bows and arrows were the major war weapons. No shields or armor were worn.

In a planned war, word was sent by messenger to the enemy, and a date for the war was chosen. Warriors painted their bodies and wore huge feather headdresses to make them look bigger than they were. Both sides sang and danced to build up a hatred for their enemy. As the lines of warriors moved toward each other, the two chiefs would move to one side of the battle field facing each other.

One by one, warriors came forward from first one side and then the other. When one man was killed, the two chiefs stopped the battle and loudly discussed the problems between the two tribes. Finally an agreement would be reached and bead money paid for the dead warrior. The tribe that had lost the warrior would declare a feast to be held in one month for the winning tribe. At this feast gifts would be exchanged and speakers from both tribes would talk of peace and of happy times ahead. Only the widow and relatives of the killed warrior were sad at such a feast.

It has been said of this tribe that it was generous to a fault, meaning the members gave to everyone who needed anything. They never bragged about their talents. The Ohlone people also believed in equal rights for all tribal members. They felt everyone should live as he or she wished as long as it did not interfere with the rights of others. The chief and council were advisers to the village to make sure equal rights were always given to all.

If problems came up in the village, a chief would usually lecture to the people who could not agree. A chief almost never handed out punishment. He was careful to keep himself well-liked. Sometimes, when a chief became too bossy, the villagers would move to another village in their territory and leave the bossy chief behind.

Children were prized and loved by tribal members. When a new baby was due, the whole village would make ready to accept its birth. After the baby was born, both mother and child were taken to a cold stream where they bathed together.

While they were bathing, the new father went into his house and dug a long hole in the floor. He lined the hole with rocks, which he then set afire until the rocks were warm. Then he removed the hot ashes with a rake and piled herbs on top of the warm stones to make a soft, warm mattress. The mother and baby stayed in this warm bed for nearly a week.

A cradle was made after the baby's birth. It was thought that making a cradle before a child was born would bring bad luck. The new cradle was lined with soft cattail fluff. The baby was then wrapped in a rabbit-skin blanket with its arms held straight against its body. A baby stayed in the cradle for about two years and was only unwrapped a few times a day for bathing and changing. A baby's ears were pierced shortly after birth.

Ohlone children were taught to not be different from others. The important thing was to obey all tribal laws and not to have the freedom to choose what each wanted to do. Children had to understand the many ways they were bound to the tribe's ancestors and Ohlone ways of life. Children were not hit or punished a great deal, but parents were very firm with them about learning good Ohlone behavior.

After age two, when the children could walk and talk, they joined with other village children and played with them until eight or nine years of age. Toys, such as acorn buzzers and acorn tops, were favorites. Children also loved to play cat's cradle with string made from plant fiber. When a child lost a baby tooth, it was buried in a gopher hole for luck.

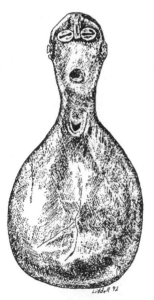

Children learned about nature and how to do adult chores by following older village children. By age eight the boys were separated from the girls. Boys learned how to make hunting weapons and to hunt. Girls learned how to gather and prepare food.

There were ceremonies when boys and girls became teenagers. Girls were tattooed on their faces, chest and shoulders in colors of blue, black or green. Tattooed designs on a girl's face were symbols of her tribelet.

Pottery doll, perhaps for a small child; hollow with a few small pebbles inside.

Later, when girls were married and moved to their husbands' village, the face tattoos told everyone to which family they belonged.

The children of chiefs usually had a marriage arranged for them by the parents. Ordinary villagers could pick their own mates. After the wedding ceremony, the groom stayed at the bride's home for a short time. He had to be careful not to look or talk to his new mother-and father-in-law. It was thought to be an insult if he did. He stayed at the in-laws' home until he had shown them that he was a good hunter, could make fine weapons, and work hard.

After a few months of proving himself worthy to the bride's parents, the groom took his new bride to his own village to live. She was then taught the ways of the groom's family. If there was a divorce, the children stayed with the mother.

Old people were treated with great respect. Tribal members listened to their older people, admiring their wisdom and all they had done. The chief made sure all old tribal members got plenty of food and excellent care.

When a tribal member died, the body was burned on the day of death. If a body was buried, it was only because there were no villagers around to gather enough wood for such a large fire, or the dead had been an important person. Most or all of the dead person's belongings were burned or buried with the body.

If the dead person was a married man, his widow always cut off her hair in mourning. Sometimes a knife was used to cut the hair, but often hair was burned off with a hot coal from a fire. Faces and heads of relatives were covered with ash or charcoal. A widow stayed in mourning for one year after her husband died.

The dead were believed to go to a land across the sea known as the Island of the Dead. Dead peoples' names were not spoken aloud until the name was given to someone else. It is thought that mourning ceremonies probably were held every year for all those who had died during the past year.

TRADE

Visitors who came to trade with the Ohlone people were treated as honored guests. The chief and other important members of the tribe painted themselves and entertained the traders with a feast cooked by the chief's wife.

The traders showed what items they had brought after the feast had been eaten. When the chief had made a choice of what he liked, he would bring out strings of shell money. The shells were all small, polished and the same size. Each string had been measured around the hand of the chief and were all the same length. The trader measured these lengths against the tattoo marks on his arm.

The Ohlone tribe loved to trade. They mostly traded with the Plains Miwok, Sierra Miwok and the Yokuts. Olivella shells were traded to the Sierra Miwoks. Ohlone traders also offered mussels, salt, abalone shells, and dried abalone from the ocean to both the Sierra Miwoks and the Yokuts.

One of the foods the Ohlones wanted was piñon nuts. Yokut people gladly traded these for ocean products the Ohlones had to offer.

Chert and obsidian flaked easily into thin slices of rock with sharp edges. Tools such as knives or arrow points, that had to have sharp points or edges, were best when made from this kind of stone. Chert was not as hard a flaking stone as obsidian, but many tribes used it for making their tools. Since chert was found in Ohlone territory, it made an excellent item for the Ohlone people to use in trade for things they wanted.

Cinnabar was a mineral mined right in Ohlone territory. It was a popular trading item with other nearby tribes, for it was used to make red body paints. A tunnel nearly one hundred feet long was discovered in the middle 1800s in the mountains near where Oakland is today. The tunnel had been dug by Ohlone people through the centuries to remove cinnabar.

Wars had been fought through history over which tribe had the rights to mine cinnabar. Stories have been told of how Native American people of the tribes living up on the Columbia River area had traveled south, from what is today Washington and Oregon, to Ohlone territory just to trade for cinnabar.

RELIGION AND MYTHS

The sun was an important part of the Ohlones' belief in a higher spirit. In fact, Sun might have been the most powerful thing in the whole universe to the Ohlone people. Sun was welcomed every morning with shouts or songs of joy. Prayers were said to the sun as smoke was blown to the sky to carry the message.

Small feathered charms were worn to make the spirits bring good luck during hunting and fishing trips. Shell beads were given as offerings to the gods and spirits to keep them happy. There were holy places outside of the village where people could leave gifts of beads, food or prayer sticks as offerings to please the gods. Usually these holy places were in quiet spots, and it was felt that very powerful spirits lived there.

Dreams played a large part in the Ohlone beliefs. Tribal members felt dreams gave them the chance to pass out of their ordinary world and into the spirit world of animal-gods. They felt dreams were real, so if an animal-god appeared in a dream and told the dreamer something, it was thought to be true fact.

Ohlone people believed that dreams could tell the future. If a person dreamed of a bird going into a house, or dreamed that a dog howled near a house, these were bad omens. It meant there was trouble ahead. When someone dreamed of a great horned owl, it was felt that a death was about to happen.

Ohlone myths tell of how Eagle, Coyote and Hummingbird created a new race of people after a great flood covered the whole earth. Falcon, Lizard and Bear were also part of the myths told by tribal members to their children. These animal-gods were not all-perfect or all-powerful but were more like humans. They made mistakes and had good and bad things happen to them. Because they made mistakes, they could teach humans how to act when a man or a woman had a problem.

A village shaman was felt to be closer to the spirit gods than ordinary village people. Villagers felt shamans could control the weather, such as stopping or starting rain, and that shamans could cure sickness. Those shamans who were trained in curing sick people used herbs, singing, and dancing to try to draw out the poison of disease from the body of a sick person.

The curing doctor of one tribelet wore a flicker (bird) feather headdress and a skirt of crow or raven feathers when dancing away a sickness. His face and arms were painted, and he wound a live snake around his arm. He glued baby bird feathers onto his face and sang, yelled and danced while leaping through fire. It was felt he could cure many diseases in this way.

Other shamans performed dances to find out from the spirits if there would be good crops of acorns, or if many fish would be caught on a fishing trip. Most tribe members really did believe the shamans could tell of the future.

Grizzly-bear shamans were thought to be masters of witch-craft. Some of this kind of doctor wore bear skins and carried bear teeth and claws filled with poison. One Ohlone tribelet believed that bear doctors could even kill relatives or people in distant villages. Often this kind of doctor would be killed himself because of his own desire to kill other people.

Shamans meant power. It was believed their power came from the animal-gods, and that some of this power could be given to ordinary people if they were good and minded the Ohlone laws.

There were many dances to the animal-spirit-gods. One tribelet had not only curing dances, but a devil's dance, a Coyote dance, a Bear dance and a Dove dance. Most tribelets had Coyote dances. As in other California tribes, Ohlone dances could last for days, sometimes for a week. Ohlone people loved to dance, fortunately.

Feathers made colorful decorations for dancers' bodies and for headdresses. More color was added to a dance when men colored their skin with charcoal dust, red clay or chalk. Ornaments were worn on the heads, in the ears, and around the necks of dancers. Women decorated themselves, too, but their colors were not as bright as those of the men dancers.

CLOTHING

When not dancing, the Ohlone people wore little or no clothing. Women wore aprons of netting or braided tule and grass. Their back aprons were usually of buckskin or sea-otter skin. Boys and men usually went naked, sometimes covering their bodies with mud to keep warm. But in cold weather, both men and women wore robes made of rabbit skin, sea-otter skin, or duck feathers sewn on buckskin. These robes were tied under the chin with a piece of fiber cord or string. The robes became blankets at night.

Men went barefoot and wore no hats. Their hair was long and either braided or tied atop the head with a buckskin

Chest tattoos of an Ohlone woman. Note chin tattoo, which tells others to what family she belongs.

thong. Sometimes their hair was cut to only about four to five inches long. Most men pulled out their face hairs with wooden tweezers or two mussel shells, so they would not have a beard. But some did have mustaches, and a few even had flowing beards. Men could be seen wearing hairnets made of milkweed fiber. Often they wore stone and shell charms around their necks. Ears and noses were pierced and often a small animal bone was worn in the nose.

Women wore bangs with the rest of the hair hanging free. They also went barefoot like the men. Tattoos of lines and dots decorated their chins, and they wore necklaces of shells and feathers. They wore grass or flowers or earrings in their pierced ears.

FOOD

The Ohlone tribe was one of only a few California Native American tribes which planted vegetables for food. Like the Achumawi (A choo ma wee) tribe of northern California, the Ohlones kept control of weeds on their land by burning the fields each autumn. Burning made annual seed-bearing plants produce many more plants the following year, and kept large amounts of dead plants from building up. Too much dead growth meant there might be a chance of fire, started by lightning, growing into a big wild fire. Native Americans greatly feared a wild fire.

One of the most important reasons for burning a field was to create a grassy meadow so deer, elk and antelope would come to graze. With animals coming into Ohlone territory, the tribe would be sure to have meat for winter food.

Even though the vegetables they planted were needed for food, the most important plant food the tribe members ate was not planted but gathered each year from oak trees: acorns. There were four kinds of oak trees which gave them acorns. Coast live oak and valley oak had the most acorns each year. The tanbark acorn was thought to have the best taste, however, and its nut meat had a whiter color. If not enough of these three acorns could be found, the acorns of the black oak were gathered, but they were not the tribes' favorites.

Acorns were ground into meal and leached to take out the bitter taste. See the first chapter of this book to find out how acorn meal was leached. Some tribes made acorn bread by wrapping balls of cooked mush in alder leaves and baking them.

Nuts of the California laurel tree were eaten raw or cooked. Hazelnuts were also eaten and enjoyed. Pits of the holly-leafed cherry were ground into a tasty food. A number of plant seeds were roasted by tossing them with live coals or hot stones in basket trays.

Wild berries such as blackberries, elderberries, strawberries, and gooseberries were favorites for summer meals, and cider was made from manzanita berries. Wild grapes were found during the summer also.

Many kinds of roots were eaten or made ready for storing for winter food. Wild carrots, two kinds of wild onions, cattail roots, as well as other roots, were eaten.

Young shoots (new branches) of three kinds of clover were gathered for salads. Not only clover, but poppy, tansy mustard, and the very tender young leaves of milkweed were eaten. Pollen dust from the all-important tule plant was collected, rolled into balls and baked. Another favorite food was the seed of the tiny redmaid plant. Even thistle plants were eaten.

When all the seeds had been gathered from a field, it was set afire in just such a way as to gather all the grasshoppers into one spot. Roasted grasshoppers were a real treat to Native Americans.

Mushrooms were collected if there was a rainy winter, and salt came from dried seaweed.

Meat from many fish and animals was enjoyed at mealtime. Black-tailed deer, elk, antelope, grizzly bear and mountain lion were all hunted for their meat. Coastal tribelets ate meat from sea lions and from whales which became beached on the sand. The meat of both sea lions and whales had a lot of fat in it. Fat was needed in the Ohlone diet to keep bodies warm in wintertime, so this fatty meat was much desired.

Smaller animals such as wildcat, skunk, raccoon, rabbit, squirrel, mouse and mole were eaten when larger animals were not found. The most important birds hunted were usually water fowl. Canadian geese and mallard ducks were especially enjoyed at mealtime. Doves, robins, quail, and hawks were eaten, but some birds such as eagles, owls and ravens were never eaten for religious reasons.

Steelhead salmon, sturgeon and lamprey eels were the fish most popular with the Ohlone people. Sometimes shark, sardines and trout were caught and prepared. Tribespeople living on the Carmel River were most fond of lamprey eels.

All kinds of snakes were eaten, but frogs and toads were not considered food.

HUNTING

Malcolm Margolin, in his book "The Ohlone Way," explains how it was thought to be very bad luck for a hunter to speak or even look at a woman before a deer hunt. A hunter also was careful not to eat certain kinds of food while getting ready for a hunt; in fact, he ate only enough food to barely live. He spent days in the sweathouse cleansing his body and his mind so as to be a successful hunter. He painted proper designs on his body and saw to it that his bows and arrows were in perfect shape for killing deer.

A hunter could go alone to hunt deer, or he might work within a group to kill the animals. When the men worked together, they could drive many deer into nets, over cliffs, or into traps where other hunters waited to kill them. More deer could be killed when the men hunted this way.

Deer hunters like to use a real deer head on their own heads so they could get closer to deer without being noticed. An explorer once wrote that the hunter he watched moved so much like a deer as he crept toward a herd, that the explorer could not tell the hunter from the animals.

A hunter would return to his village with great pride after he killed a deer, but he did not eat his own meat. That would be a show of bad manners to the rest of the village and the spirits would be angry with him.

A Native American deer hunter hunted deer reverently. Although he did not pity the deer when he killed one, he did have great respect for the animal and was grateful to it. Ohlone hunters knew how important the deer were to their people. Deer gave them warm deerskin clothing for cold weather, bone from antlers for tools, sinew for hunting weapons, and meat for meals. Every part of a deer was used in some way. Nothing of the animal was wasted.

Hunters knew that antelope were always thirsty, so they would go in groups to an antelope watering place. Tying strips of animal skin to their arms and ankles, some of them would lie on their backs and wave their arms and legs in the air. When an antelope came to look closer at what strange things they were seeing, a hunter hiding nearby would shoot the animal with bow and arrow.

Ducks and geese were caught with nets and decoys. Decoys were duck or goose skins stuffed with straw to look like live birds. These decoys were placed by hidden nets and when live birds came near the net was pulled over them.

Cage-like traps made of twigs might be used to capture quail, or sometimes a bola would do the job better. A bola was a piece of strong string with a small bone tied to each end. The string was held at one end and swung over the

Duck hunting, using decoys to draw ducks toward a net trap.

head. When a good hunter let go, the string could fly a long way into the air and wrap itself around a bird.

Sounds could also be used to draw animals near. Rabbit hunters knew how to suck hard against their fingers to make a noise like a scared or trapped rabbit. Other animals, as well as rabbits, would come to see the imaginary animal in trouble and were killed themselves. There were also hunters who could actually smell certain animals when they were near.

FISHING

Shellfish were collected in baskets by women as they searched the beach for food, but men did all the catching of fish. Sturgeon and salmon were caught in seine nets or dip nets. Often a weir was built across a stream to catch fish. A weir was a woven fence with only one narrow opening in it. Fish had nowhere to swim but through the opening. A basket trap was placed at the opening and the fish were trapped as they swam through.

Spears would be used when catching larger fish. Often fishing was done at night. Fishermen lit torches to attract the fish and then speared them or scooped them up in nets as they came into view.

TOOLS AND UTENSILS

Nets were made of string which came from the fibers of the milkweed stalks. Stalks were made into fiber by men of the village because they had the strongest fingers and fingernails. Fingernails were run down the stalks until the pulp (soft part) was scratched away, leaving the fiber of the stalk. With his left hand a man would feed the fibers onto his upper leg while rolling them together with his right hand, criss-crossing them to make a thin rope. This type of cord was very strong. Many fish were caught in nets made of tough milkweed cord.

Having a fine bow was the most important goal of Native American men. It sometimes took a hunter ten days to make a bow perfect enough to suit him.

Bows for deer hunting were about four feet long, flattened in the center, and tapered at both ends. There was a rounded hand grip in the middle. Thick pieces of otter or weasel fur were wrapped around the bow about six inches from each end. Strips of deer sinew were glued to the back of the bow. This made the bow more bendable, or flexible.

It was best not to string the bow until an animal was in sight. Keeping the wood bent all the time would make the bow not as flexible and the arrows would not travel as far as the hunter wished. Good hunters could string a bow as they ran toward an animal.

A hunter also kept his bow very clean. He rubbed deer marrow into the wood to make his bow look shiny and beautiful. Men would trade seafood or salt to other tribes for what they felt was the best wood for making a bow, because a good bow was any man's most prized possession. Wood the Ohlone hunters liked best for their bows came from a mountain forest belonging to another tribe.

Ohlone hunters used many kinds of arrows. Probably the best arrow central California tribes made was a two-piece one which had a main shaft of cane (a dried hollow reed) trimmed with hawk feathers but had no point. At one end the cane was dug out to form a pocket. Into this pocket was fitted another, smaller shaft called a foreshaft. This foreshaft was made of hardwood and had a sharp point of flint or obsidian tied and glued onto it. Each hunter painted his arrows with his own pattern, so he could tell his from arrows of other hunters.

Arrows had to be straight if they were to go where the

hunter wanted them to go. All hunters used a grooved piece of rock, usually steatite, to straighten their arrows. When an arrow bent, a hunter would heat the steatite until it was hot, then roll the arrow shaft around and around in the groove of the rock to straighten it. Not only were stones used to straighten arrows or as arrow points, they were used as net sinkers, anchors for boats, smoking pipes, and cooking tools. You already read about cooking tools in the section titled Food.

Useful minerals were found in the mountains around the San Francisco Bay area. One of the main uses of these minerals was creating colorful body paints. From hematite and cinnabar came red paint. White paint was made from clay.

Awls are sharp-pointed tools that were used for marking the sides of wood or stone bowls, or for making holes in leather or wood. They were a much-needed tool. Ohlones made them out of either bone or wood.

Brushes were made from the roots of the soap plant. These brushes were what the women used in preparing acorn meal. Wooden paddles were made for stirring food. Shells made excellent spoons.

When the hair of an animal had to be removed to make soft skin clothing, the women used an animal rib bone to do the scraping, or "fleshing", as it was called.

Several different kinds of mortars and pestles (long tools for grinding and mashing) were used by Ohlone women in preparing grains. Most mortars were stones small enough to be carried, with one flat side. Some stone mortars were part of a huge rock and could not be moved. Wooden mortars could be hollowed out from a log. Pestles might be either stone or wood.

Small mortars with wooden pestles were used for grinding seeds to make paints or herbs for medicine. When hard grains or seeds were being mashed, a basket without a bottom was glued to a mortar so bits of grain would not fly into the wind.

BASKETS

Ohlones made some of the finest baskets the world has ever seen. They were an all-important art to Ohlone women, but basket art was always useful art because baskets were needed in every part of Ohlone life. Seed-

Coiled basket with tiny shell bead decorations.

beater baskets were made so seeds could be shaken from plants. Seeds and acorns were winnowed, parched and sifted with baskets. Some baskets were so tightly woven they could carry and even store water. All boiling of food was done in basket pots. Small baskets made good dippers and mush bowls.

Large baskets were used for collecting plant foods, for preparing foods, and for storing not only food, but belongings. One large cone-shaped basket was called a burden basket. It was worn on the backs of women when they had a heavy load to carry. What would the Ohlone women have done without baskets?

Today there are only about a dozen original Ohlone baskets left for us to see. Most of them are tattered from use and old age. Some can be found at the University of California, a few at Mission San Juan Bautista, some at the Santa Cruz City Museum, some at the Los Altos Public Library, and there are even two baskets in Russia, one in Paris, France, and one is in the Smithsonian Institute in Washington, D.C.

MUSIC AND GAMES

Music was usually a part of religious rituals and myths. Singers chanted rhythm songs while the dancers performed ritual dances. People watching the dances clapped their hands. Split-stick rattles and bird-bone whistles would add to the excitement of sounds. As the dancers stamped their feet on the ground, they felt they were getting rid of problems and building a new and better world.

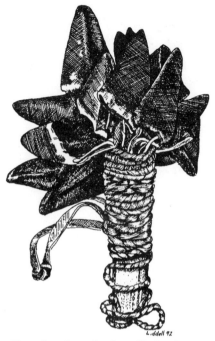

Deer hoof rattle; handle is of vegetable fiber rope; about 11 inches high.

Songs were sung for good luck in hunting trips. Songs were sung as love charms. Along with split-stick rattles, which were made of laurel wood, cocoon rattles were used for rhythm. These were made by attaching cocoons to wooden handles.

Although not many musical instruments made musical tones, the Rumsen tribelet is known to have played some wooden whistles. Flutes made of alder wood and blown from the end, have been found. Some whistles were carved out of tiny bird bones. The only stringed instrument seems to have been a musical bow, which was played by pulling the string with fingers.

Shinney was a popular game the Ohlone people liked to play. In this game a wooden puck was struck with curved sticks to try to reach a goal at the end of the playing field. It might have been an ancient form of hockey.

There was also a ball race played in which a wooden ball was kicked along a marked course. One contest was called the hoop-and-pole game. The object was to throw a spear through a moving hoop.

Women enjoyed games using dice and other kinds of hand games. As you read under Village Life, children had hunting contests, played hoop-and-pole, cat's cradle, and hide-and-seek.

A loser never complained, but kept a smile on his/her face. The winner never bragged. Adults and children alike remembered the teachings of the Ohlone way of behavior which was to not show hurt or pride, no matter what a person did.

HISTORY

The first white explorers the Ohlone tribe saw were from Spain. In 1602, Sebastian Vizcaino landed in the Monterey Bay area. The Rumsen tribelet met the boat, and was written about in the explorer's journal. Nothing more seems to have been written about the Costanoan-Ohlone tribe until 1769, when Spanish missionaries arrived. Those missionaries, and the explorers who came with them, wrote a great deal about the Native Americans already living there.

Between 1770 and 1776, seven missions were founded. Mission records show that the last of the original Ohlone tribelets had disappeared by 1810, as Ohlone tribespeople entered into mission life.

Ohlone people had never been around diseases the Spaniards brought with them. When they were exposed to measles, small pox, and other kinds of sicknesses, they had no immunity. Almost 8,000 mission Indians died in the next sixty-five years. By 1835, only 2,000 Ohlones were left.

When Mexico took over the missions from the Spanish monks, the mission Indians suffered in many ways. Spain had promised the mission farm lands to their mission Indians. Instead, Mexican military officers took the land for themselves and, in many cases, made the mission Indians work as laborers and slaves in their farm fields and homes.

The United States took over the California territory in the middle 1800s. Unlike other tribes, Ohlone tribes were not given any reservation lands. Groups of Ohlone people gathered together in small villages near Monterey, San Juan Bautista and Pleasanton. No government money was paid to them for schools or health care. The United States government also did not pay Ohlone people for land the tribes lost during Gold Rush days when miners came onto Ohlone land and stayed.

By 1935 no living person spoke the Ohlone languages, and the last full-blooded Ohlone died in the 1980s. A recent survey showed that of known tribal members living in the Bay area today, none of whom are full-blooded, no one is without a job. The old Ohlone way of living still holds true: Work hard, do not complain, always behave in a good way.

OHLONE TRIBE OUTLINE

I. Introduction
    A. Population before mission days
    B. Tribelet villages
        1. Languages spoken
    C. Explanation of Costanoan and Ohlone names
    D. Territory
        1. Boundary markers
        2. Tribal lands today

II. The village
    A. Sizes of villages
    B. Description of houses
        1. Materials used
        2. Size of house
    C. Sweathouse
        1. Description and uses
    D. Dance and ritual area
    E. Assembly house
        1. Shape and size
        2. Location
    F. Granaries — description

III. Village life
    A. Work done by men and women
    B. Chief
        1. Why chief had largest village house
        2. How chief was chosen
        3. Chief's wealth
        4. Jobs of Chief
            a. War Chief
            b. Description of war
        5. Chief's council
        6. Settling village disputes
            b. Why chief did not give out punishment
    C. Ohlone tribal traits
    D. Newborn tribal customs
    E. Older children's training

GLOSSARY

AWL: a sharp, pointed tool used for making small holes in leather or wood

CEREMONY: a meeting of people to perform formal rituals for a special reason; like an awards ceremony to hand out trophies to those who earned honors

CHERT: rock which can be chipped off, or flaked, into pieces with sharp edges

COILED: a way of weaving baskets which looks like the basket is made of rope coils woven together

DIAMETER: the length of a straight line through the center of a circle

DOWN: soft, fluffy feathers

DROUGHT: a long period of time without water

DWELLING: a building where people live

FLETCHING: attaching feathers to the back end of an arrow to make the arrow travel in a straight line

GILL NET: a flat net hanging vertically in water to catch fish by their heads and gills

GRANARIES: basket-type storehouses for grains and nuts

HERITAGE: something passed down to people from their long-ago relatives

LEACHING: washing away a bitter taste by pouring water through foods like acorn meal

MORTAR: flat surface of wood or stone used for the grinding of grains or herbs with a pestle

PARCHING: to toast or shrivel with dry heat

PESTLE: a small stone club used to mash, pound, or grind in a mortar

PINOLE: flour made from ground corn

INDIAN RESERVATION: land set aside for Native Americans by the United States government

RITUAL: a ceremony that is always performed the same way

SEINE NET: a net which hangs vertically in the water, encircling and trapping fish when it is pulled together

SHAMAN: tribal religious men or women who use magic to cure illness and speak to spirit-gods

SINEW: stretchy animal tendons

STEATITE: a soft stone (soapstone) mined on Catalina Island by the Gabrielino tribe; used for cooking pots and bowls

TABOO: something a person is forbidden to do

TERRITORY: land owned by someone or by a group of people

TRADITION: the handing down of customs, rituals, and belief, by word of mouth or example, from generation to generation

TREE PITCH: a sticky substance found on evergreen tree bark

TWINING: a method of weaving baskets by twisting fibers, rather than coiling them around a support fiber

NATIVE AMERICAN WORDS
WE KNOW AND USE

PLANTS AND TREES
hickory
pecan
yucca
mesquite
saguaro

ANIMALS
caribou
chipmunk
cougar
jaguar
opossum
moose

STATES
Dakota – friend
Ohio – good river
Minnesota – waters that
　reflect the sky
Oregon – beautiful water
Nebraska – flat water
Arizona
Texas

FOODS
avocado
hominy
maize (corn)
persimmon
tapioca
succotash

GEOGRAPHY
bayou – marshy body of
　water
savannah – grassy plain
pasadena – valley

WEATHER
blizzard
chinook (warm, dry wind)

FURNITURE
hammock

HOUSE
wigwam
wickiup
tepee
igloo

INVENTIONS
toboggan

BOATS
canoe
kayak

OTHER WORDS
caucus – group meeting
mugwump – loner politician
squaw – woman
papoose – baby

CLOTHING
moccasin
parka
mukluk – slipper
poncho

BIBLIOGRAPHY

Cressman, L. S. *Prehistory of the Far West.* Salt Lake City, Utah: University of Utah Press, 1977.

Heizer, Robert F., volume editor. *Handbook of North American Indians; California, volume 8.* Washington, D.C.: Smithsonian Institute, 1978.

Heizer, Robert F. and Elsasser, Albert B. *The Natural World of the California Indians.* Berkeley and Los Angeles, CA; London, England: University of California Press, 1980.

Heizer, Robert F. and Whipple, M.A.. *The California Indians.* Berkeley and Los Angeles, CA; London, England: University of California Press, 1971.

Heuser, Iva. *California Indians.* PO Box 352, Camino, CA 95709: Sierra Media Systems, 1977.

Macfarlen, Allen and Paulette. *Handbook of American Indian Games.* 31 E. 2nd Street, Mineola, N.Y. 11501: Dover Publications, 1985.

Margolin, Malcolm. *The Ohlone Way.* Box 9145, Berkeley, CA 94709: Heyday Books, 1978.

Murphey, Edith Van Allen. *Indian Uses of Native Plants.* 603 W. Perkins Street, Ukiah, CA 95482: Mendocino County Historical Society, © renewal, 1987.

National Geographic Society. *The World of American Indians.* Washington, DC: National Geographic Society reprint, 1989.

Tunis, Edwin. *Indians.* 2231 West 110th Street, Cleveland, OH: The World Publishing Company, 1959.

Weatherford, Jack. *Native Roots.* 201 E. 50th Street, New York, NY 10022: Crown Publishers, 1991.

Credits:
Island Industries, Vashon Island, Washington 98070
Dona McAdam, Mac on the Hill, Seattle, Washington 98109

Acknowledgements:
Kim Walters, Library Director, and Richard Buchen,
Research Librarian, Braun Library, Southwest Museum
Special thanks